This book is dedicated to all who find Nature not an adversary to conquer and destroy, but a storehouse of infinite knowledge and experience linking man to all things past and present. They know conserving the natural environment is essential to our future well-being.

DENALI

THE STORY BEHIND THE SCENERY®

Interpretive captions by Don S. Follows

Don S. Follows, a former park planner and interpretive geologist whose field studies, writings, and photography defined national significance for 17 new parks in the Southwest and Alaska, provides the captions.

Text adapted from the previous edition of *Denali: The Story Behind the Scenery.*

Denali National Park and Preserve *located in Alaska, north of Anchorage, was established in 1917 to protect North America's highest mountain, Mt. McKinley, and wildlife.*

Front/Back cover: Mount McKinley from the north side, photo by Jeff Gnass. Inside front cover: Caribou on a tundra ridge, photo by Kim Heacox. Page l: Dall sheep ram, photo by John P. George. Page 2/3: West Branch of the East Fork of the Toklat River from Polychrome Pass, photo by Jeff Gnass.

Edited by Mary L. Van Camp and Cheri C. Madison. Book design by K. C. DenDooven.

Ninth Printing, 2004 • Revised Edition

DENALI: THE STORY BEHIND THE SCENERY © 1997 KC PUBLICATIONS, INC.

*N*atural processes undisturbed by humans
and repeated since creation weave
the rich fabric of the Denali ecosystem.

FRED HIRSCHMANN

Shaped by centuries of ice, blanketed by persistent snows, and soaring in a 650-mile-long arc of monolithic mountain majesty, the Alaska Range commands the headwaters of its mightiest rivers—the Yukon, Susitna, and Kuskokwim. Frequent earthquakes speak of a land still in the making.

At the apex of the arc in southcentral Alaska is the mighty Mount McKinley massif—centerpiece of Denali National Park and Preserve, and North America's highest mountain. For centuries, people have been attracted to the region's dynamic scenery and abundant wildlife— bear, sheep, moose, and caribou—which roam freely through cold and remote settings. Here, we witness wild landscapes, and watch dynamic struggles of life and death in a subarctic ecosystem.

Indescribably beautiful, the Denali wilderness tests the scope of physical endurance and often provides supreme adventure.

Spring snowmelt provides habitat for migrating waterfowl. Beyond is Mount Mather, named in 1947 for Stephen T. Mather, the first director of the National Park Service.

5

The Mountain

The Athabascans, who long ago made Alaska their home, have always called the 20,320-foot-high mountain *Denali*—"the high one." Today, it is more commonly known as Mount McKinley, and is without question the most impressive feature of the Alaskan landscape. It occupies the focal point in a region rife with geologic activity and interest. The mountain and the range above which it looms are but parts of a continental system of mountains and uplifting forces, the Cordilleran system, which extends from South America north through the United States, through Canada, into Alaska, past McKinley, and then to the Aleutian Islands. The geologic events that have taken place here have resulted in a country of unusual beauty, where wide, low plains contrast with icy peaks and domes of somber magnitude.

The 650-mile-long mountain chain, known as the Alaska Range, passes through the park and forms a natural land barrier between the coastal lowlands around Anchorage, Alaska's most populous city, and the northern interior. On its western side this range forms a drainage divide where rivers flow west to the Bering Sea or south to the Gulf of Alaska. Most of its peaks are less than half McKinley's height—McKinley and nearby Mount Foraker stand in remarkable isolation.

The range lies on the Denali Fault System, the largest crustal break in North America, stretching 1,300 miles across Alaska's full width, passing through the park and separating Alaska's most ancient rocks from those much younger.

Having adopted the "plate tectonics" theory, geologists now believe that sections of the earth's crust are not stationary—they are in fact

PETER KRESAN

mobile, and their drifting movements account for most of the geologic changes that occur at the earth's surface. In the case of McKinley, this force has produced a rise from Wonder Lake in the 2,000-foot lowland on the north to the 20,320-foot summit—one of the highest and most spectacular vertical rises of any mountain on earth, including those in the Himalayas.

Slanting skyward from its tectonic △
*apex in the southcentral Alaska Range
and rising 20,320 feet above sea level, the
Mount McKinley massif stands tall and
timeless, dominating everything within its
shadow of influence and controlling human
perspectives since time immemorial.*

GLACIERS AND GLACIAL ACTION

Denali National Park and Preserve lies at
the northern edge of the ice-age glaciation that
covered most of the northern hemisphere and
retreated between 10,000 and 14,000 years ago.
(It may be a surprise to many that much of that
part of Alaska which lies north of the park was
not covered by this continental ice sheet.)

Numerous ice flows still radiate from the
highest peaks of the Alaska Range, where temper-

atures never get high enough to melt them. Such is the case with McKinley, so that, gazing at the mountain from a distance, one sees not a dull, gray monolith, but an exciting sculpture in ice. Over a core of slate and granite, an irregular sheath of snow and ice has spread itself like a mantle reaching down for about 14,000 feet—a mantle that may be hundreds of feet thick in places.

Past glaciers, too, have left their chiseled paths, by cutting rounded cirques and valleys and knife-edged ridges. Today's glaciers creep down these valleys like viscous rivers, or adhere to the sheer ridge faces. Ice falls and crevasses break the whiteness where glaciers change the angles of their slopes or modify the rates of their flow. *Bergshrunds*—crevasses that separate the moving ice from the stationary ice—rim glacier-filled cirques and make them appear like bowls of shrinking, drying pudding.

At the lower edge of the Harper Glacier, which rests between the mountain's north and south peaks, is the Harper Icefall. Looking deceptively like a still-life waterfall from where we view it, the icefall empties ice in an awesome 800-foot plunge to the upper Muldrow Glacier, where the ice continues its sluggish travel to the lowlands and the dark, rubble-laden terminus of the Muldrow, within a mile of the park road.

The Muldrow Glacier has surged twice in the last 100 years—most recently in the winter of 1956-57. The middle section of the 32-mile-long glacier flowed rapidly—the upper end sank 200 feet, leaving a "high-water" mark on the canyon walls and, at its lower end, the glacier heaved countless tons of ice and rock into ragged piles. In 1986-87, the Peters Glacier, just to the west, surged about 3.5 miles.

Evidence of glacial action is abundant in the lowlands as well. Eskers (ridges of coarse gravel) and moraines (boulders, stones, and other debris) mark the paths and termini of ancient glaciers, and most rivers are laden with glacial silt (rock that has been ground to a powder by the moving ice upstream). Here and there are erratics (huge boulders) that were carried to and dropped at their present positions by glaciers now diminished or gone.

PETER KRESAN

▲ *Glaciers are frozen rivers of ice which move down alpine valleys with slow-motion but powerful force and rhythm. Along their long, sinuous paths they pluck valley walls clean and carry rock waste many miles to the glacial terminus. During its transport downslope, rock and gravel debris, accumulating along the path of destruction, is seen as medial or middle moraines and as side or lateral moraines. Glaciers are grand sculptors of the earth, forming some of the most magnificent mountain scenery in the world.*

△ **Cathedral Spires are a massive cluster of granitic rocks displaying sculpted scenes of classic** *glacial erosion. Located in the southwestern region of the preserve, the massive spires have been chiseled by an ice age which left behind knife-edge ridges on vertical walls standing high above the Susitna Lowlands. They were named in 1898 by J.E. Spurr of the U.S. Geological Survey during early explorations into the vast region. Mountain-building forces and the action of glaciers have combined to produce sharp and spectacular relief. Denali's glaciers are crystalline links between the remote past and today's striking landscapes.*

Glacial erratics are large boulders ▷ *avalanched onto ancient glaciers, transported far beyond their source and deposited alone on foreign soils after ice sheets melted and left them stranded. Smaller debris of the glacial moraine, such as gravel, sand, and silt, eventually weathers and combines with organic materials to form crude soils. A glacial erratic always stands alone in stark testimony to another time and another place of origin.*

JEFF GNASS

GALEN ROWELL/MOUNTAIN LIGHT

Climbers discover first-hand the harsh physical environment on Mount McKinley.

ED COOPER

CLIMBERS CHALLENGE THE MOUNTAIN

McKinley is not, by most routes, a technically difficult climb, but thin air combined with extremely low temperatures (a thermometer left at 14,500 feet in 1913 and found undisturbed 19 years later registered more than 95° below zero!) and furious winds gusting up to 150 mph make it a foremost challenge. The low air pressures and temperatures on upper slopes have startling effects upon the human body—dehydration sets in, appetites fade, headaches pound, sleep comes but sparingly, strength wanes, and judgment fails.

The first attempt to climb McKinley was made by Judge James Wickersham and his hand-picked team of four men and two mules. They departed on May 16, 1903, "with flags flying and the dance hall band [playing]" and, after traveling to McKinley's base, began the climb on June 20. They found themselves not equal to the task, however, and upon reaching 8,000 feet on the northwestern slope they turned back.

Dr. Frederick Cook, a highly regarded veteran polar explorer, tried from the south in the same year, but got only 3,000 feet higher than Wickersham before he, too, turned back. Cook was determined to succeed and in September 1906, he and Edward Barille, his horse packer, made a brief and mysterious journey from Cook Inlet back to the mountains. The two returned 12 days later, claiming they had reached the top.

Cook's account, with summit photograph, was published nationally and his accomplishments were widely lauded. But his claims were disputed from the first, and the controversy they sparked was to occupy headlines and countless columns of type for years to come. In 1910, three attempts were made to prove or disprove the story. Finally, a group sent by the Explorers' Club of New York located the peak upon which Cook had taken his "summit" photos—an unnamed ridge 11 miles southeast of McKinley and only 5,300 feet high!

◁ **Mountaineers must have fortitude, endurance,** and skill. Modern climbing techniques and equipment have vastly improved over crude equipment fashioned from wood, canvas, and fur nearly 100 years ago. Time has not changed the same physical barriers of ice, altitude, and weather which face all challengers. Regardless of careful preparation and planning, Mount McKinley still claims victims each year!

△ *A weary climber rests at a site below the summit of Mount McKinley, looking south and west towards Mount Foraker and Mount Hunter. Moisture-laden clouds from the upper Cook Inlet to the south move into distant valleys 18,000 feet below and begin to stack up against the mountain massif. Added hours of summer daylight allow mountaineers to work around the clock. Many climb at night to avoid glaring snow and blinding sun.*

Such controversy only fueled the heated opinions of the people of Fairbanks who had contempt for outsiders climbing "their" mountain. Believing that McKinley could be climbed—and that Alaskans should be the ones to do it—a local climbing party was organized and funded. Four miners, toughened men used to the hardships of trail conditions, were drafted for the honor—Pete Anderson, Billy Taylor, Charles McGonagall, and leader Thomas Lloyd—later affectionately known as the "Sourdoughs."

The party mushed off by dogsled from Fairbanks in late December of 1909, reached Cache Creek in February 1910, and established a base camp from which they located and ascended a new route to the Muldrow Glacier, a route that proved to be much easier than those previously tried. Upon reaching 11,000 feet, three of them—Anderson, Taylor, and McGonagall—left for the final ascent, outfitted with their crude, home-made equipment and toting a thermos of hot chocolate and a bag of doughnuts for lunch. McGonagall dropped out at the 18,500-foot level, but the other two waltzed up and back down the final 10,000 feet in a single day, April 3, packing a flag and 14-foot spruce flagpole that they planted on the North Peak (19,470 feet—850 feet lower than the South Peak), for the people of Fairbanks 150 miles distant.

This was a feat hardly to be credited. (Even today, from the same 11,000-foot level, climbers must plan on at least two weeks to reach the top.) Doubts were again cast as the purported flagpole could not be seen from Fairbanks. Controversy raged once more, and the Sourdoughs' claims were generally discounted.

In 1912, two more unsuccessful attempts were made. Finally, in 1913, success came to a four-man party led by Harry Karstens (who later became the first superintendent of Mount McKinley National Park). At about the 15,000-foot level one of the party peered toward the North Peak and saw, to the great joy of all, a flagpole perching near the summit! The Sourdoughs' claims were true, after all. Reaching the long-sought destination on June 7, it was perhaps fitting that Walter Harper, an

ED COOPER

▲ *Moving past a large ice and snow* cornice, which overhangs the ridge upon which it formed, a lead climber is roped up to avoid a possible slip and tumble down the steep slope.

Alaskan native, was the first to set foot on the true summit of McKinley, also known as the South Peak, at 20,320 feet above sea level.

Today, most of the over 10,000 people of 30 nationalities who have stood on the summit started from the 7,000-foot level, to which they were flown by ski plane. Nylon and aluminum equipment and vacuum-dried foods have replaced the crude tools and doughnuts carried in 1910, but accidents and illnesses are frequent, and helicopters have often plucked the sick and injured from the mountainside—saving them from situations that may have been fatal even as late as 25 years ago.

The mountain has provided a majestic stage for these and other human endeavors since 1903, and the evidence left by these adventurers is apparent to anyone who has traversed its popular routes. But the healing properties of avalanches, glacial surges, and blowing snow are great—the mountain remains seemingly untouched, serene in its regal indifference to the frantic activity that people have brought to its icy slopes.

The Climb
An account by Ralph Tingey

Our ascent was up the West Buttress route of Mount McKinley. It was a bright daylight morning. We left our tents at 0300 hours to begin the longest trek we'd ever recall. Winds were blowing hard. The temperature was 17° below zero. New snow covered previous tracks ahead. We felt alone on top of the world. Glancing off a thin ridge to 18,000 feet below, we could see clouds stacking against lower mountain peaks and drifting upward toward us.

The higher we climbed, the slower we climbed. Each footstep took its toll on our minds and bodies. Hearts pounded in our chests! Strong sun glared off fresh snow! Winds bit hard into our sluggish progress! Taking five deep gulps of thin air for each step forward, we trudged along deliberately, ever onward, ever upward toward our goal.

Suddenly, strong winds died. Clouds rose and enveloped us with a warm mist. The temperature rose to 30° above zero. We were capsuled in a warm air bubble which followed us to the summit. Still ahead was the final ridge—one slip here, and gravity would dash our bodies 10,000 feet down the South Wall into the shrouded depths below. We inched along.

Soon, we were all standing on top of Mount McKinley! The euphoria of mountain conquest overwhelmed us. We quickly sat down and gave each other traditional handshakes. The agony, hard work, and aching lungs and legs became secondary as we viewed scenes of incredible vastness and solitude.

We celebrated those cherished moments on the summit of North America's highest peak, but dared not linger. It would be a long way back and only one direction remained—down! On our descent, miles slipped by effortlessly. The many thousands of feet, which had taken us over one week to ascend, disappeared behind us in just a couple of days.

But the memories remain—of Mount McKinley, the greatest adventure of our lifetimes!

SUGGESTED READING

BROWN, WILLIAM E. *Denali—Symbol of the Alaskan Wilderness: An Illustrated History of the Denali-Mount McKinley Region, Alaska.* Virginia Beach, Virginia: The Donning Company Publishers, 1993.

COLLIER, MICHAEL. *The Geology of Denali National Park.* Denali Park: Alaska Natural History Association, 1989.

MOORE, TERRIS. *Mt. McKinley: The Pioneer Climbs.* Seattle, Washington: The Mountaineers, 1981.

WASHBURN, BRADFORD. *Mount McKinley: Conquest of Denali.* New York: Harry N. Abrams, 1991.

The Many Moods of McKinley

JEANNE DRAKE

JOHN CONRAD

TOM WALKER

▲ **A**lmost lost in a scenic backdrop of massive mountains, a shallow lake on the southern border reflects

FRED HIRSCHMANN

◁ **F**rozen monoliths of the Alaska Range stand above shimmering shelves of ice and snow. During late spring, heavy snow accumulations can plunge as avalanches from thin, mountain ridges down dizzy depths to glacier cirques tucked below. The scenery of South Denali has been formed by south-flowing alpine and valley glaciers. These tend to have far longer lengths than glaciers found on the northern side, which are smaller and less active. Scenic flights over this southern domain spell out the complexities of the tumultuous terrain.

oth Mount Foraker (on the left) and Mount McKinley (to the right).

△ **An icefall plunges from a higher valley onto the surface of Ruth Glacier. Icefalls impose** formidable challenges to climbers who attack such frozen walls and undulating seracs with crampons, hammer, and ice axe. Standing in bold contrast is a wall of granite known as the Shield, the height of which is equivalent to a 15-story office building.

The vegetation present in the park attests mutely but dramatically to the strength of the forces of cold air, permafrost, brief summers, and mountainous topography.

Taiga and Tundra

The area that now lies within the park had virtually no vegetation 14,000 years ago—valleys were flooded with ice, and mountaintops protruded from the glacier sheets. To the north was an ice-free area that extended to the southern slopes of the Brooks Range, carpeted with prairie-like grasses and populated by large mammals. To the south and east lay thick ice and bare rock. To the west, a broad, ice-free isthmus—the Bering Land Bridge—provided access to and from the Old World.

Today, the valleys are empty of ice, save for the small, rock-strewn glaciers at the heads of some rivers. The mountains stand clear from their bases to their summits, but hanging glaciers or perennial snow patches still cling to their flanks. Silty rivers gush from melting glaciers and wind across flat gravel bars, cutting at the banks.

Over limited areas a layer of thick topsoil may be found, but although it is rich in organic material few plants can survive. Soils of this sort are found where drainage is poor—often overlying permafrost (soil that has been frozen for perhaps centuries) that is found in vast areas of Alaska. It is in such areas that the frozen carcasses of ancient mammoths and bison have been found.

Most visitors to Alaska view plant life during the growing season of less than 100 days. The

JOHN CONRAD

◁ **"To stroll** the autumn tundra's glow and find a quiet pond where reflections of the mind and soul take dreaming far beyond..." Solitude, scenery, and splendor can be discovered when you seek your own space.

△ **The taiga forest stirs in the morning shimmer of a late summer sunrise. Fog banks and** *mist rise in unison after a night of rainfall. Too soon, beads of water on grasses and shrubs will turn to morning frost as leaves begin to splash autumn colors.*

450 species of Denali's trees, shrubs, and herbs spend most of their lives in physical and metabolic dormancy, but during the brief summer they work frantically to ensure their survival.

THE TAIGA

Taiga is a Russian word that describes a woodland or forest of the Far North. In Denali, this forest is an assemblage of evergreen trees interspersed with deciduous trees of modest size including aspen, balsam poplar, and paper birch. Within older, well-established woodlands, white and black spruce are predominate taiga trees.

The floor of the white-spruce forest is covered with a variety of low shrubs, herbs, and lichens. Many of these are also present in black-spruce woodlands, but most of the ground there is covered with sphagnum and sedges.

In some areas heavily saturated with water, soils slip over the underlying permafrost, and

△ **Tussock tundra is often waterlogged and** *difficult for hikers to negotiate. The soft, uneven humps, often surrounded by water at their base, seem endless after a long day of hiking.*

ED COOPER

17

the trees of the taiga lean comically and tipsily in all directions, giving rise to the phrase "drunken forest."

The Tundra

Above the timberline (about 2,700 feet in Denali) the taiga gives way to the tundra both *moist* and *dry*—windswept, treeless slopes where the vegetation may include shrubs, sedges, herbs, mosses, lichens, or a mixture of these. The spruce-forest/moist-tundra interface is a picturesque one and biologically very significant, since it supports the colorful variety of wildlife that is a major feature of the park.

Dominant plants of the moist tundra are dwarf birch, willows, or other shrubs, which form a knee-to-waist-high growth that is fairly closed. The ground beneath and between these shrubs is covered with combinations of many of the same plants found on the forest floor. Tundra shrubs create a colorless realm of dark, dry, twiggy stems most of the year when the subarctic twilight encloses the area in darkness for up to 20 hours a day. Then, as sunlight reaches its maximum of

By middle August, fresh snows △ strike the Alaska Range. Cold nights paint rich amber gardens which radiate in brilliant crimson, yellow, purple, and orange.

Treeless ridges, tundra valleys, shallow ponds, and sinuous river channels form typical landscapes where permafrost, cold air, mountain topography, and ▽ brief summers control a world of extremes.

KIM HEACOX

△ **Shrubby cinquefoil hugs a cold, windy** ledge of an ancient rock, where lichen and moss break down rock surfaces and build pockets of crude soil which other plants will invade.

LARRY ULRICH

△ **Tundra supports a complex mixture of miniature** plants. Bearberry, crowberry, mosses, blueberry, lichens, dwarf willow, and birch, along with varieties of delicate wildflowers, form typical tundra mats.

19 hours toward the middle of June, the transition from gray sticks to verdant "shrub meadow" is startlingly abrupt.

By early August, tundra shrubs already show signs of senescence. Colors fade and a few leaves turn to amber. By the end of August, tundra shrubs are turning to orange, yellow, and crimson as leaves die and chlorophyll fades. As abruptly as it came to life, the moist tundra reverts to a leafless tangle of twiggy stems and settles down for a frigid metabolic rest.

At elevations above 3,400 feet the prevailing vegetation is *dry* or *alpine* tundra which consists mostly of plants that attain a height of only three or four inches. Growing in clumps or mats on rough, rocky soils, they merge to cover the red-brown soil with a plush, green carpet—the most pleasing to the eye of all Denali's vegetation types.

Tundra plants at their highest elevations in the Alaska Range are among the hardiest vanguards of the subarctic biota. The upper limit of all vegetation here is approximately 7,500 feet.

The vegetation present in the park attests mutely but dramatically to the strength of the forces of cold air, permafrost, brief summers, and mountainous topography. Tundra swale in midsummer may seem lush, productive, and pasturelike, but a boot heel can easily cut through the illusion, exposing the coarse rock rubble that has given slow birth to what is actually a very fragile, thin, green mantle. On a dim, frigid December day the same tundra slope presents a very different impression, but one that is vastly more realistic.

Life here is a series of winters, bounded by June and August.

SUGGESTED READING

HULTEN, ERIC. *Flora of Alaska and Neighboring Territories.* California: Stanford University Press, 1968.

PRATT, VERNA E. and FRANK G. *Wildflowers of Denali National Park.* Anchorage, Alaska: Alaskakrafts, 1993.

VIERECK, LESLIE and ELBERT L. LITTLE, JR. *Alaska Trees and Shrubs.* Anchorage: University of Alaska Press, 1986.

▲ *In the far northern woodland or boreal forest a mosaic of colorful patterns is seen among* autumn displays of yellow and gold painted by willow, aspen, birch, and poplar trees. The somber green of white and black spruce dominates.

▲ **Announcing an early frost, an aspen stand flares skyward.**
*Its golden leaves are contrasted against crimson-colored shrubs
entering the autumn parade. Following wildfires, fast-growing aspen
stands develop in upland areas on south-facing slopes.*

▲ **Old man's beard hangs from branches**
*of a fallen birch tree. It can be found on cooler,
northern sides of white spruce trees and
thick vegetation where sun-shaded, moist
conditions attract rapid growth. Lost explorers
used the lichen's north-facing preference as
a crude compass.*

The
Taiga

White spruce, ▷
*willow, and dwarf
birch form extensive
shrub thickets which
attract moose and
caribou. Within
Alaska's taiga forest,
mature stands older
than 200 years are
rare because of
wildfires which burn
vegetation every 50
to 150 years.*

The Tundra

△ **Usually found in damp areas at lower elevations,** the pale corydalis is a pioneer plant which builds soils for less-tolerant species destined to arrive later.

△ **A bumblebee pollinates monkshood, a** poisonous plant which prefers to grow in moist alpine meadows and along running water.

◁ **White fields of Alaska cotton or cotton grass** wind along saturated water channels towards the distant, ermine peaks of Mount McKinley.

TOM WALKER

KIM HEACOX

TOM WALKER

△ **P**ink and white forms of fireweed occur, but most plants are dark, reddish-pink in color. Fireweed grows in burned-out areas and open fields, and along river bars.

Willow catkins are signs △ of spring! Favorite browse of moose, Alaska willows number at least 33 species.

Silky-haired glacier avens survive on rocky slopes, close ▽ to the warm ground where they evade cold winds.

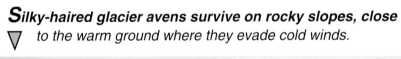

STEVE MCCUTCHEON

Red dwarf fireweed △ and white bearflower grace the side slopes of a tumbling brook, which emerges from beneath a melting snowfield.

Overleaf: A canoe on ▷ Wonder Lake is dwarfed by the commanding presence of Mount McKinley. Photo by Tom and Pat Leeson.

23

Denali has the distinction of being a wildlife community that is intact. All of the native plant and animal species are present, and no species have had to be reintroduced.

Wildlife of the North

The vast wilderness that is Denali National Park and Preserve enables a spectacular array of wildlife to live together in a sustained, natural balance. This delicate web of life encompasses 37 mammal species and 157 bird species. There are no snakes or lizards, but one amphibian, the elusive wood frog, is sometimes seen in the Wonder Lake area.

 Winter offers the greatest challenge subarctic animals must face—they must, for the most part, either hibernate or leave as most birds do. Some animals take advantage of the anonymity offered by Denali's winter landscape. The weasel, ptarmigan, and snowshoe hare exchange their

ED COOPER

△ **Sounding a series of high-pitched** whistles, a spotted sandpiper faces strong spring winds.

Pursuing ▷ the scent of a favorite meal, a grizzly bear prepares to dig out a ground squirrel burrow. These large land predators prey on caribou and moose for major protein needs, but are primarily grazers.

HARRY M. WALKER

26

brownish summer-tundra coats for white ones, and the Dall sheep are completely at home.

Only about 20 of the park's bird species spend their winters here—the other 137 travel south to the far corners of several continents. In summer the scene changes rapidly and dramatically, and the bird life of Denali becomes a truly cosmopolitan community. The subarctic is an important breeding area for birds of North America, and by June a variety of species can be found in every habitat. Frozen ground and permafrost have resulted in lakes and ponds, ideal habitats to support waterfowl and shorebirds. Summer also brings hordes of insects, which plague wildlife and humans alike, but provide a staple diet for many small birds.

Denali's several plant zones support bird and mammal communities that are somewhat distinct from each other. Some animals, typically carnivores, do not restrict themselves to a particular vegetation zone, but travel widely in search of specific food items—wolverines and red foxes are prime examples.

On high mountain ridges, where Dall △ *sheep are safe from most predators, a group of resting rams survey all directions from their sunny site. These white, thinhorn sheep are widely scattered throughout Alaska and are unique among North American mountain sheep species, all of which have excellent vision, remarkable climbing skills, and massive, curled horns.*

TAIGA WILDLIFE

The lowland taiga forest is home to a community of animals who have adapted to its soft, light snow, little or no wind, and the particular plants it offers. Moose, while taiga animals, often prefer the taiga/moist-tundra interface at the treeline and, occasionally, are found far above timberline where their long legs aid them in traversing deep snow.

The snowshoe hare and its predators form a distinct subcommunity within the taiga. Throughout the Far North, hares undergo drastic and regular fluctuations in their numbers, com-

Blending with ▷
the seasons, a
short-tailed weasel
benefits as both
hunter and the
hunted. The white
fur or ermine winter
phase of the coat
changes to
brown in summer.

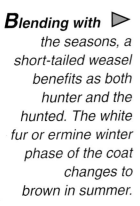

TOM & PAT LEESON

NATIONAL PARK SERVICE PHOTO

Wolves interact with many species. By preying on ▷
sick and aging animals, wolves help maintain the
natural vigor of moose and caribou populations in the park.

On large, padded ▷
feet which provide
traction over deep winter
snows, a Canada lynx
catches its preferred
prey, the snowshoe
hare. Lynx are the only
cat native to Alaska.

JEANNE DRAKE

RON LEVY

JOHN P. GEORGE

◁ **A** willow
ptarmigan, Alaska's
state bird, stands
poised for swift retreat.
Its color variations
from summer brown to
winter white hide it
well within the varied
Denali landscape.

◁ **A**n arctic ground squirrel carries
dry grass to its burrow. Ground squirrels are
food for grizzly bears, wolves, and eagles.

Moving in annual migrations in search △
of lichen and vegetation, caribou require large territories over which to graze. Winter vegetation is reached beneath snow with wide, front hooves and the "shovels" at the base of the caribou's antlers. The park was expanded in 1980 to include additional habitat for its declining caribou herd.

pleting a cycle of population changes every 10 or 11 years. During the low phases of this cycle, they are scarce to the point of rarity, but at the high points the forests seem to be alive with them. The fortunes of animals that are dependent upon hares as food, such as lynx, goshawks, and coyotes, are closely linked to this cycle and build their numbers a year or two after the rabbit population has started to climb.

TUNDRA WILDLIFE

In shrub-tundra (moist-tundra) zones, the wildlife is generally inconspicuous and unspectacular, except for the moose and caribou sometimes seen here, and the grizzlies that are attracted when berries ripen. Tiny rodents (voles and lemmings) attract northern harriers, short-eared owls, weasels, and foxes. Small passerine birds, including three species of sparrow, are abundant in summer, feeding upon birch catkins, insects, and the many varieties of seeds available here in autumn and spring.

Caribou, although not specifically limited by moist-tundra boundaries, are often observed here

in the summer. Well-known for their nomadic lifestyle, caribou undergo yearly movement patterns that have been repeated in Denali, with some variations, for as far back as there are records.

Today, the caribou population of the park is but a small remnant of the 25,000 resident animals in 1940, while populations of Dall sheep, grizzlies, and moose have either grown, fluctuated insignificantly, or remained stable. What happened to the caribou? In all of the park's history, this is perhaps the most perplexing wildlife question to arise. The decline does not appear to have been caused by human factors and intensive studies suggest that it may reverse itself in time.

Some of the most picturesque and intriguing of Denali's animals dwell in the alpine-tundra

△ *A* **grizzly bear sow and her new cub wander across a tundra meadow. The female's tender** care and watchful concern for her offspring is demonstrated by the protective instincts which she displays with vigor when danger comes near. Blond fur is a common phase for Denali bears, but colors will vary with individuals from light to dark brown. The food of a grizzly is mostly plant material. Alaska is the home of 98 percent of the United States' grizzly bear population.

FRED HIRSCHMANN

JOHN P. GEORGE

△ *High* **bush cranberry is** only one of the many species upon which bears feed.

△ *With* **a playful nature that is always alert to danger, a grizzly rolls** in the grass. Temperaments vary with individuals. One moment a grizzly can seem playful and indulgent, while in the next instant it can become a ferocious killing machine. Note the long claws used for digging out rodent burrows and ripping apart fallen prey.

▲ ***A** coastal grizzly or brown bear searches for salmon. Coastal grizzly bears, feeding on plentiful runs of spawning salmon, are much larger than Denali's interior grizzlies.*

areas—Dall sheep, white-tailed ptarmigan, hoary marmots, pikas, and arctic ground squirrels live year-round among its rocky outcroppings and talus slopes. Dall sheep make short seasonal migrations from the ridges of the Outer Range north of the park, where they live during the winter, to the main Alaska Range, an important summer range.

THE PREDATORS

Grizzly bears occupy an unusual position in the Denali ecosystem, and they present many paradoxes—the reasons, perhaps, that they are of such great interest to visitors. Although often seen lumbering about, grizzlies have incredible speed for short distances, allowing them to be fairly effective predators of caribou, young moose, and ground squirrels. They also feed on new shoots of grasses and flowering plants, and consume an incredible amount of berries in late summer and fall.

At Denali you can observe the truly remarkable grizzlies living, breeding, playing, and feeding just as they did hundreds of years ago.

The large size of the park, and the wilderness character of surrounding lands, provide the prey and the land base needed for a thriving grizzly bear population.

Among the mammals whose ranges are not tied to a particular vegetation type, the largest and best known is the wolf, which has long been the object of much public attention and scientific curiosity. So it was that biologist Adolph Murie spent the years from 1939 to 1941 in what was then Mount McKinley National Park, examining the relationships of wolves to sheep, caribou, moose, and other species. He concluded that, although wolves were indeed killing and eating sheep and other animals, they could not be considered a scourge—rather they were a beneficial and very important element of the ecosystem. His report, *The Wolves of Mount McKinley,* has become a classic of American wildlife writing.

Many national parks have interesting wildlife, but Denali has the distinction of being a wildlife community that is *intact.* All of the native plant and animal species are present, and no species have had to be reintroduced.

KIM HEACOX

△ **D**all sheep rams move up the ridge to a high meadow. Mountain sheep occupy alpine ridges and steep slopes adjacent to extremely rugged terrain, where they flee to elude predators.

Dall sheep rams practice their sparring △ techniques which help establish the social order of the band. Clashes can occur throughout the year. They are more frequent and serious during fall breeding when large rams engage other rams with similar horn size. Dall sheep are not only the embodiment of the Denali spirit, but a major reason for originally establishing Mount McKinley as a game refuge in 1917.

SUGGESTED READING

MCINTYRE, RICK. *Grizzly Cub: Five Years in the Life of a Bear.* Portland, Oregon: Alaska Northwest Books, 1990.

MURIE, ADOLPH. *The Grizzlies of Mount McKinley.* Seattle: University of Washington Press, 1987.

MURIE, ADOLPH. *Mammals of Denali.* Denali Park: Alaska Natural History Association, 1983.

MURIE, ADOLPH. *A Naturalist in Alaska.* Tucson: University of Arizona Press, 1990.

MURIE, ADOLPH. *The Wolves of Mount McKinley.* Seattle: University of Washington Press, 1987.

⚠ **Cow moose meets bull moose in the romantic setting of Wonder Lake! Moose breed** in September and October. Calves are born in mid-May and early June. Calf twins are not uncommon, and cows will defend their newborn vigorously. Predation by wolves and grizzly bears often takes one of the twins before maturity. Moose have a high reproductive potential and will quickly fill a range unless predation or severe weather conditions reduce populations.

JOHN CONRAD

◁ **A bull moose** feeds on vegetation in shallow ponds, on leaves of willow, birch, and aspen. This long-legged, heavy-bodied male with the drooping nose and dewlap under his chin can wade far from shore. In prime condition by fall, this male moose can weigh between 1,200 and 1,500 pounds. Moose are the largest member of the deer family in the world.

33

◁ *A beaver chews on a willow branch close to its den, which is made from branches and serves as a food cache. Adult beavers weigh 30 to 50 pounds and are North America's largest rodent.*

⚠ **A red fox carries a ground squirrel** and a ptarmigan to its hungry offspring waiting in a grass-lined den in the side of a distant knoll. Fox will eat muskrats, squirrels, hares, eggs, birds, vegetation, and carrion. Wildlife should never be offered food by well-meaning, but uninformed, park visitors.

⚠ **The red squirrel is the noisy** chatterbox of the coniferous forest and spends summers cutting and storing green spruce cones for winter.

***A** hoary marmot keeps an* ▷
ever watchful eye near its burrow
at the base of a talus slope,
the rocks of which not only provide
protection from predators,
but make good lookout stations.

△ *An alert dweller of rocky terrain, the*
northern or collared pika prepares to sound its
shrill bark.

Covered with hair and sharp ▷
quills which protect it from enemies, the
porcupine's poor eyesight makes
"porky" rely on its strong sense of smell.

No time to be on a narrow stream bank! A wolf retreats upstream from sleeping grizzly bears that
have gorged on a bull caribou carcass. Grizzlies will defend their rights and return later to feed on fallen
▽ *prey. This sometimes means driving off other Denali predators, such as fox, wolf, and even wolverine.*

◁ *The arctic tern is* *a champion migratory species in Alaska, traveling over 20,000 miles between the Arctic and the Antarctic. It is commonly observed hovering over a pond and diving for small fish.*

△ *Seen soaring over mountain ridges in search of prey, golden eagles have wing spans reaching seven feet.*

A beautiful, red-throated loon nests ▽ *on the island shore of a shallow lake.*

△ *The American kestrel is a small falcon* *which nests in tree cavities and hovers over meadows with a rapid beating of its wings.*

GRIZZLY BEAR

THE ROLLING TUNDRA BEYOND IS THE TYPICAL SUMMER HOME OF THE GRIZZLY BEAR. LIKE MOST BEARS, THE GRIZZLY IS AN OPPORTUNIST - THOUGH ITS MAIN DIET IS MADE OF SUCCULENT PLANTS AND BERRIES, IT CAN OFTEN BE SEEN DIGGING FOR GROUND SQUIRRELS, OR RARELY, CONSUMING A KILL OF MOOSE OR CARIBOU. CUBS, BORN BLIND AND NAKED IN SNUG WINTER DENS, ARE CARED FOR BY THE PROTECTIVE SOW FOR THREE YEARS. WHEN THE MATING URGE IS AGAIN UPON HER SHE WILL RUN OFF HER CAPABLE OFFSPRING. ADULT BEARS IN ALASKA'S INTERIOR MAY WEIGH 600 POUNDS AND CAN RUN FASTER THAN 35 MPH. DO NOT APPROACH OR ATTEMPT TO FEED THEM. REMEMBER, YOU ARE IN THE ANCESTRAL HOME OF THE GRIZZLY. IT RESPECTS ONLY THE LAW OF THE WILD.

GRIZZLY BEARS ARE DANGEROUS!

Animals have fun too!

Denali's most impressive wilderness credential is its wildlife. Where else can we routinely watch grizzly families as they dig tirelessly for roots along river bars—and caribou as they peer inquiringly at us from their grazing habitats? This haven for wildlife is often referred to as the Serengeti of North America.

Animals in Denali interact with human intrusions in ways that often seem comical. Watching their behavior and antics provides great pleasure for park visitors. Just remember that wild animals have specific purposes in all they do.

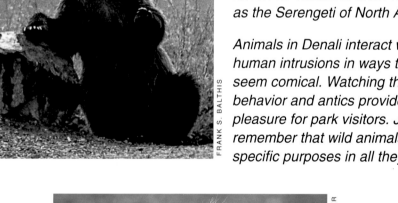

AREA CLOSED
CLOSED TO ALL ENTRY
CRITICAL WILDLIFE HABITAT

37

*In 1898, the U.S. Geological Survey traveled
to the southern foothills of the Alaska Range
with Robert Muldrow for whom Muldrow Glacier was named.
Muldrow, using only crude equipment, computed
McKinley's elevation at an amazingly accurate 20,464 feet
—only 144 feet more than its actual height.*

Those Who Came Before. . .

Long before the first European set eyes on its majestic heights, the mountain had been a central figure in the culture of native Alaskans. To them it was *Denali*, *Doleyka*, or *Traleyka* ("the high one"), according to which Athabascan tribe they belonged to. Legends of spiritual significance centered around the mountain and dominated their lives. It was where the midsummer sun set, flooding the mountain's north wall with a crimson glow. For these first Alaskans, the mountain was truly the home of the sun.

Native history is puzzlingly absent in the Denali area. It is believed that the Tanana Indians used the area but, although several archaeological surveys have combed the park, few sites of aboriginal occupation have been located. Therefore, our record of human involvement in this country must begin with the early explorers who probed it from the south.

EXPLORATION AND EXPLOITATION

The first documentation was by Captain George Vancouver, an Englishman who, in 1794, explored the Cook Inlet and glimpsed what he called the "distant stupendous mountains." For the next 90 years there is scant historical record until a Russian, Baron Ferdinand P. von Wrangell, pointed out the location of what is now Denali National Park and Preserve on his 1839 map by indicating a group of high mountains, two of

As wild and pristine as the day the first Europeans or the first American gold prospectors viewed it, ▽ *Denali's arctic tundra reaches toward mountains which fill our hearts with hope and our minds with wonder.*

△ **Long before white people set sights on Denali, the mountain was a central figure in the culture** *of Athabaskan Indians. The crimson glow of a midsummer sun flooding the north wall of Denali encouraged the belief that "the high one" was the home of the sun.*

which were mentioned by name: *Tenada* (Mount McKinley) and *Tschigmit* (Mount Foraker).

The country had not even been explored when the United States, through the foresight of Secretary of State William H. Seward, acquired Alaska from Russia for the sum of $7,200,000. This remarkable achievement was commemorated on October 18, 1867, in a flag-raising ceremony in the old Russian town of Sitka, in which the United States took formal possession.

THE LURE OF GOLD

Americans regarded "Seward's Folly" or "Seward's Icebox" as a waste of the taxpayer's money and, until the discovery of gold, the area remained unpenetrated by non-Native people. Gold, however, brought ambitious men into this rugged country—first to Cook Inlet (1896), then Dawson, Nome, Fairbanks, and Kantishna. William A. Dickey, a goldseeker, published glowing reports in the January 24, 1897, issue of the *New York Sun* in which he called the mountain he named Mount McKinley (after the recently nominated presidential candidate from Ohio, William McKinley), "America's grandest rival to Mount Everest."

In 1898, George Eldridge of the U.S. Geological Survey traveled to the southern foothills of the Alaska Range with a party of eight, including Robert Muldrow for whom Muldrow Glacier was named. Muldrow, using only crude equipment, computed McKinley's elevation at an amazingly accurate 20,464 feet—only 144 feet more than its actual height.

◁ **N**orthbound for Denali Park and Fairbanks, the Alaska Railroad train crosses Hurricane Gulch 296 feet above the stream bed. Spanned by a 918-foot trestle, the gulch crossing challenged early 20th-century engineers. This railroad, built and originally operated by the federal government, still serves as a major access route to Denali.

In the former Mount McKinley National Park, gold was never found in any paying amounts, but the area that is now part of the northern addition to the park saw a gold rush in 1905 that greatly influenced the history of the entire area. By the spring of 1906, the true extent of the gold deposits was disappointingly apparent—no more than enough to keep a few men busy for a few years. The exodus was sudden and nearly complete.

A New Breed of Adventurer

Other men were attracted to the area for very different reasons. Charles Sheldon, a Vermonter who arrived in 1906, was an impressive figure best described as a "hunter-naturalist." His keen interest in studying the wildlife of Denali (especially the Dall sheep) was blended inextricably with his passion for big-game hunting. Returning the next year, he and Harry Karstens, his packer and guide, built a log cabin on the Toklat River to serve as a base for their travels.

Sheldon conceived and vigorously implemented the drive for the establishment of a national park in the region—a need that was accentuated by talk of bringing a railroad into Alaska's interior. With the means to bring even more hunters to an already well-publicized game haven, Sheldon and others wondered what would remain of the Denali wilderness.

A Park Realized

In 1916, bills for the establishment of Mount McKinley National Park were introduced into

Wild animals are always wild! This careful sheep stalker would never attempt such foolishness with a ▽ grizzly bear or with a cow moose and calf!

The town of Talkeetna is still renowned as ▷ *the center for glacier landings along the south side of Mount McKinley, where mountaineers disembark to challenge Denali. Flightseeing is a Denali experience never to be forgotten!*

both houses of Congress and finally, on February 26, 1917, President Wilson signed the bill into law. He then handed the pen to a jubilant onlooker—Charles Sheldon.

For the first four years the infant park had few amenities. It was not until 1921 that funds to staff the park were finally provided by Congress. The man hired to be its first superintendent was Harry Karstens.

In 1938, the road was completed to Wonder Lake, and the Mount McKinley National Park Hotel—to be managed by the Alaska Railroad—was constructed. Meanwhile, the advantages of using the airplane as a means of access to the park were beginning to be realized. In 1933, a 1,000-foot landing strip was cleared to the east of the railroad tracks—it was improved and lengthened for wartime use by the army in 1943.

It was not until the 1972 completion of Alaska Highway No. 3 (Anchorage-Fairbanks) that public usage of the park increased significantly. With this event, the park was propelled into the perilous currents of civilization and was

forced to face many of the problems already dealt with by parks in more populous areas.

On December 2, 1980, President Jimmy Carter signed the Alaska National Interest Lands Conservation Act into law. The park was extended in the north, west, and south by a total of about 2,426,000 acres, with an additional 330,000 acres included as Denali National Preserve where a wider range of uses is permitted. The entire unit, officially known as Denali National Park and Preserve, is often referred to simply as Denali National Park. The name of the mountain itself, however, continues as Mount McKinley by specific action of Congress.

◁ *Kantishna Mining District Recorders Office, circa 1905. The district recorded "pay dirt" in the Kantishna Hills, but this small strike hardly supported the rush of prospectors who came, lingered, then wandered elsewhere.*

41

△ **O**nce the occasional domain of hunting parties, government explorers, fur trappers, and prospectors, the McKinley region provides a panorama of size and space still luring new generations of outdoor adventurers.

△ **N**o matter how visitors choose to tour the park, what they experience always meets—or exceeds—their expectations.

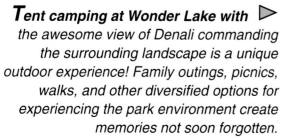

△ **W**hile mosquitoes plague both man and beast, they cannot discourage dedicated photographers who marvel at the fascinating assemblage of subarctic wildlife species scattered among stirring scenes of rich and vibrant colors.

Tent camping at Wonder Lake with ▷ the awesome view of Denali commanding the surrounding landscape is a unique outdoor experience! Family outings, picnics, walks, and other diversified options for experiencing the park environment create memories not soon forgotten.

Denali tour ▷ buses gather at Stony Hill Overlook, where passengers catch a rare and remarkably clear view of Mount McKinley.

JEFF GNASS

JEANNE DRAKE

△ **I**n a performance which delights park visitors, a bull caribou beds down for an afternoon rest.

HARRY M. WALKER

A willing Denali husky watches for a call to participate in a sled dog team demonstration. National △
Park Service rangers maintain a dog kennel and still conduct winter patrols by sled dog team. Essential inventions
for transportation in the Far North, use of dogs, sleds, and snowshoes originated with Alaska Native Peoples. ▽

KIM HEACOX

ROBERT M. BUTTERFIELD

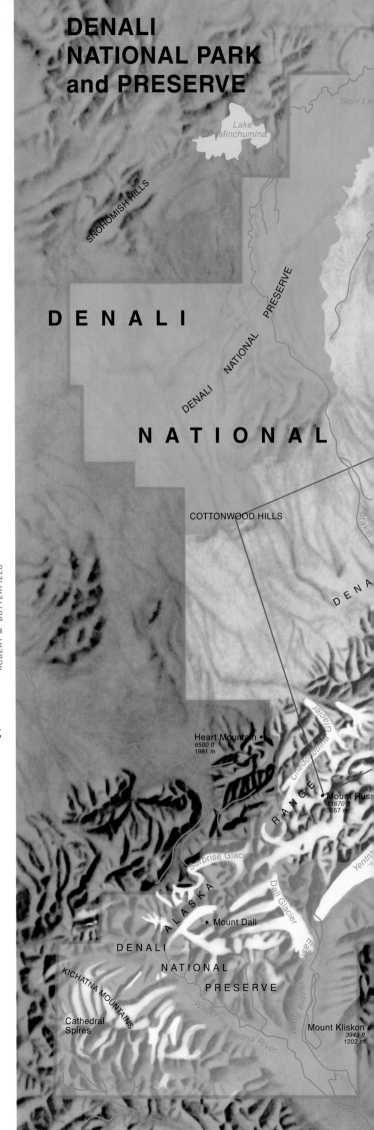

In deathlike darkness of winter, northern lights appear in drifting arcs and drapery-like patterns tinted blue, green, red, and purple. Related to sunspot activity, the aurora borealis is caused by charged electrons and protons striking gas particles in the upper atmosphere.

Denali's weather changes without warning! The annual range of temperatures is extreme, from -50°F to +80°F. Average July temperatures are a high of 62°F and a low of 43°F. Snowfalls are not unusual in any month. In the land of the midnight sun, on June 21 there are 20 hours and 49 minutes of daylight. Conversely, on December 21, there are only 6 hours and 4 minutes of daylight. Starting from 2,000 feet above sea level and rising over 18,000 vertical feet to its lofty summit, Mount McKinley is acclaimed to be the "tallest" mountain in the world.

44

Since the 1970s, Denali National Park has emerged as one of the most popular summer attractions in Alaska. In 1980, President Jimmy Carter signed into law a Denali National Park and Preserve, which expanded the park's previous size to include all the ridges leading to Mount McKinley, and extended wintering and calving grounds for the Denali caribou herd.

Viewing wildlife in their natural habitat and seeing North America's highest mountain are important to many. Denali's landscape diversity, unique wildlife, south-flowing glaciers, and hardy vegetation form a rich and wild fabric which lures tourists, scientists, and adventurers from all over the world.

What draws the visitor to this northern exposure? Perhaps it is the "wildness of it all" which teases the human spirit, a tundra terrain which challenges untrained vision and urban perspectives. For many, it is the stupendous mountain massif, which defies the arrogant and exalts the humble.

Daybreak erases cool morning mists lifting from a tundra pond, perched in an autumn-toned meadow of dewdrop jewels where moose and bear have trod.

Denali Today

The face of Alaska has changed, and the park has changed along with it. But that which meets the eye today bears a strong resemblance to the country that Charles Sheldon saw. The wilderness values are still here, enriching the lives of those who seek them.

The imprint of people has been faint. In many parts of the park the signs that usually accompany increased visitor usage are in fact imperceptible, even to the most sensitive observer. It is with much care that we must decide just what it is that we truly want from the Denali experience!

The sound of the rumble of an avalanche from a sun-rotted mountain wall, or the sight of a wolf giving futile chase to a band of caribou are rare and powerful experiences. Such moments clarify the wry distinctions between real life and fantasy. Nowhere else on earth can these experiences be had in just this way, and none can be *repeated* in just this way—even in Denali itself.

Americans and others all over the globe travel from its farthest corners to partake of the unique banquet Denali National Park and Preserve offers. The national park concept has served us well indeed in the Far North—its value cannot but continue to increase in the future.

JOHN P. GEORGE

A Dall sheep surveys the massive mountain majesty which inspires and delights humankind.

KC Publications has been the leading publisher of colorful, interpretive books about National Park areas, public lands, Indian lands, and related subjects for over 40 years. We have 6 active series—over 135 titles—with Translation Packages in up to 8 languages for over half the areas we cover. Write, call, or visit our web site for our full-color catalog.

Our series are:

The Story Behind the Scenery® – Compelling stories of over 65 National Park areas and similar Public Land areas. Some with Translation Packages.

in pictures... The Continuing Story® – A companion, pictorially oriented, series on America's National Parks. All titles have Translation Packages.

For Young Adventurers™ – Dedicated to young seekers and keepers of all things wild and sacred. Explore America's Heritage from A to Z.

Voyage of Discovery® – Exploration of the expansion of the western United States.

Indian Culture and the Southwest – All about Native Americans, past and present.

Calendars – For National Parks in dramatic full color, and a companion Color Your Own series, with crayons.

To receive our full-color catalog featuring over 135 titles—Books, Calendars, Screen Scenes, Videos, Audio Tapes, and other related specialty products:

Call (800-626-9673), fax (702-433-3420), write to the address below, Or visit our web site at www.kcpublications.com

Published by KC Publications, 3245 E. Patrick Ln., Suite A, Las Vegas, NV 89120.

Inside Back Cover: In the ▷ *magic of moonlight, Denali's commanding splendor speaks to us of silent spaces, stormy traces, and trackless places. Photo by Jeff Gnass.*

Created, Designed, and Published in the U.S.A.
Printed by Tien Wah Press (Pte.) Ltd, Singapore
Pre-Press by United Graphic Pte. Ltd

Terrific Tunes for Two

7 Exciting Duets for Elementary to Late Elementary Pianists

Martha Mier

Foreword

Something magical occurs when piano students share their music through ensemble playing! Playing duets with friends or family members is an exciting and fun aspect of piano study.

The seven duets in *Terrific Tunes for Two*, Book 1 will encourage the elementary piano student to play with imagination. Both the primo and secondo parts are written at an equal level of difficulty.

It is my sincere hope that these duets will provide much pleasure and entertainment for both the performers and the audience. So find a duet partner and have a terrific time sharing music!

Cover art: Steve Curtis

Alfred

The Old Rocking Chair

Secondo

Gently

Both hands one octave lower than written

Martha Mier

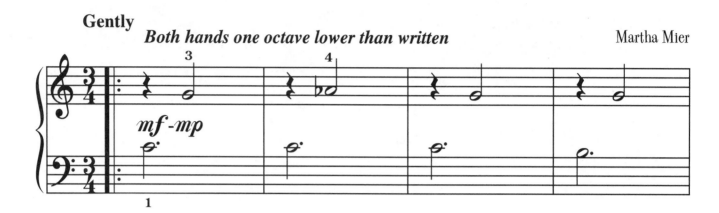

The Old Rocking Chair

Primo

Gently

2nd time both hands one octave higher than written

Martha Mier

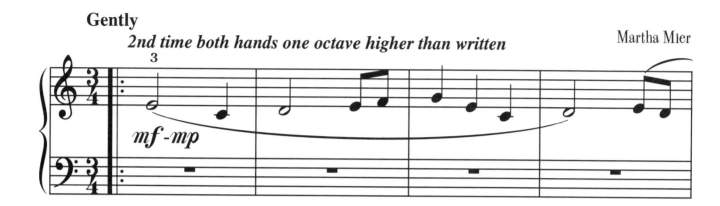

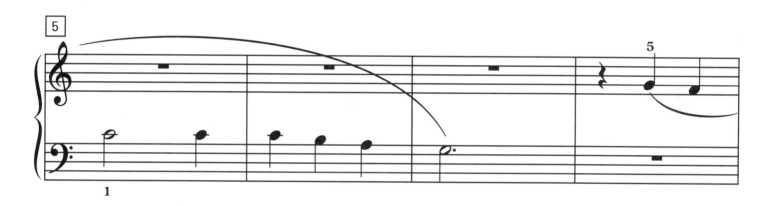

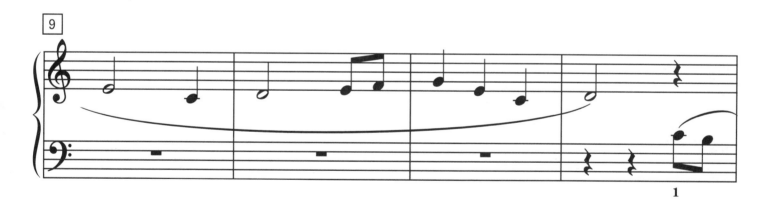

Dandelion Waltz

Secondo

Cheerfully
RH one octave lower than written

Martha Mier

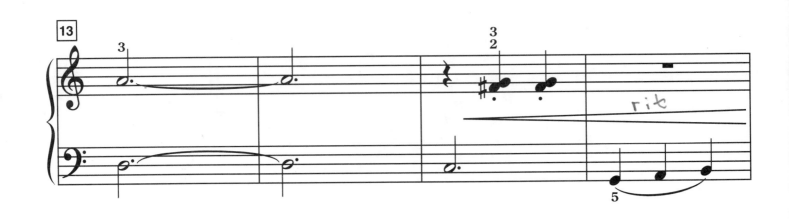

Dandelion Waltz

Primo

Cheerfully
Both hands one octave higher than written

Martha Mier

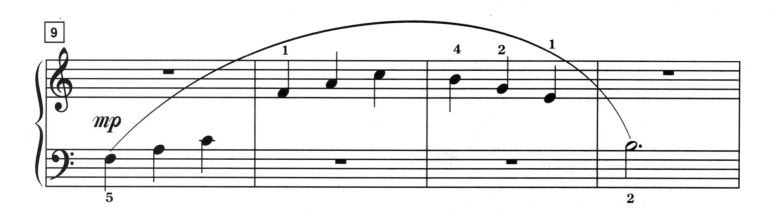

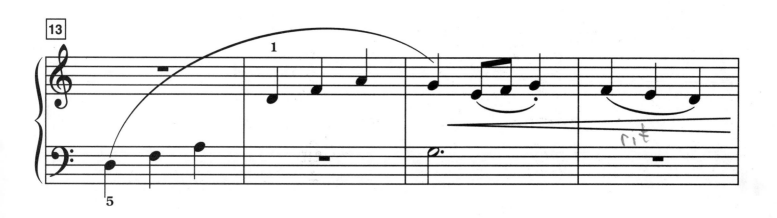

Secondo

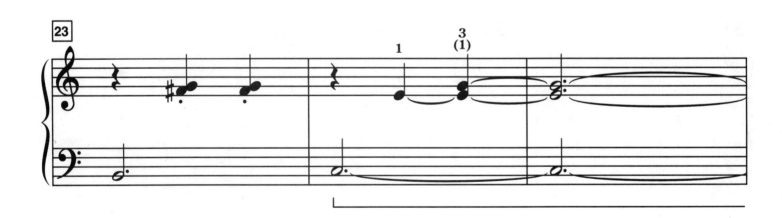

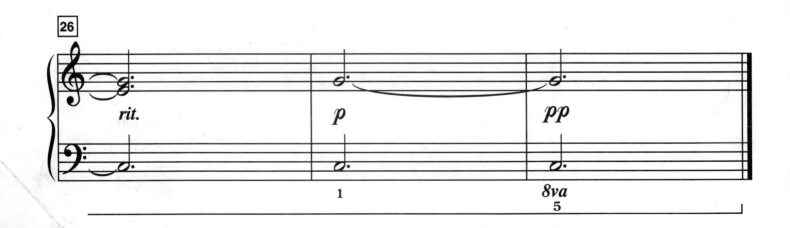

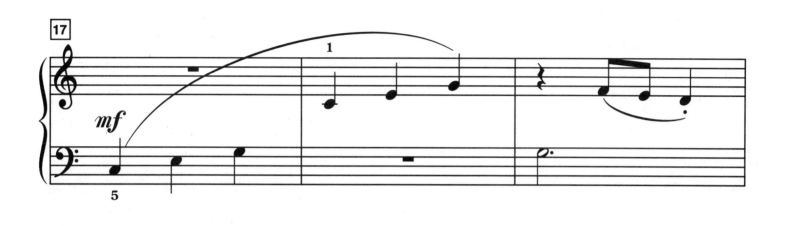

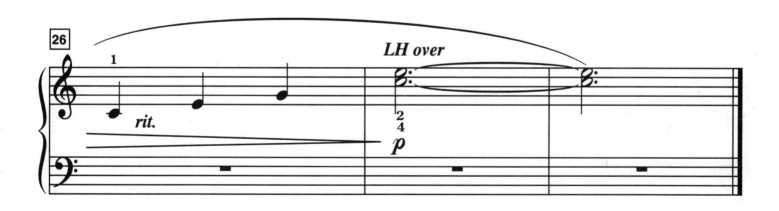

Evening Prayer

Secondo

Quietly

Both hands one octave lower than written

Martha Mier

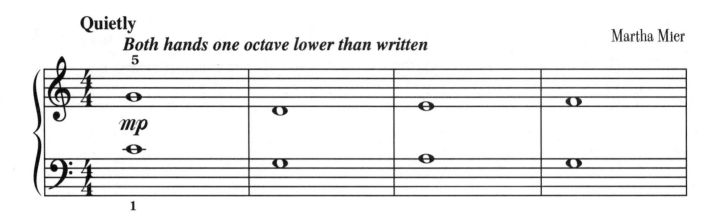

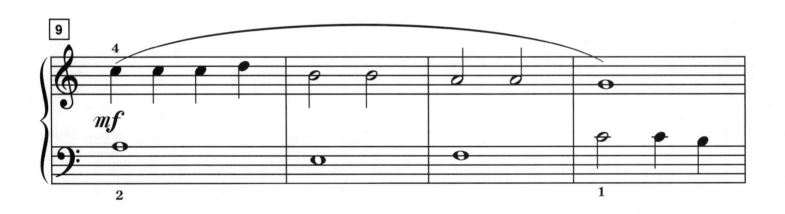

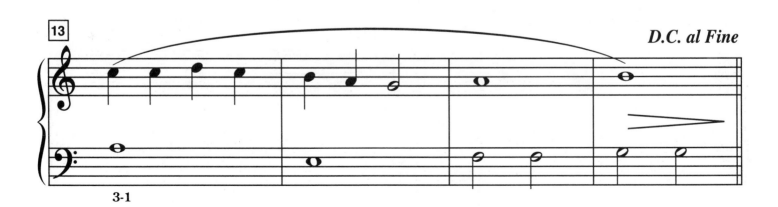

Evening Prayer

Primo

Martha Mier

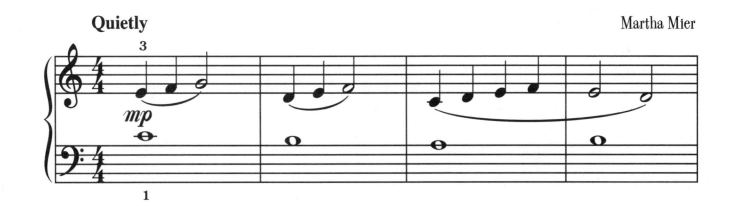

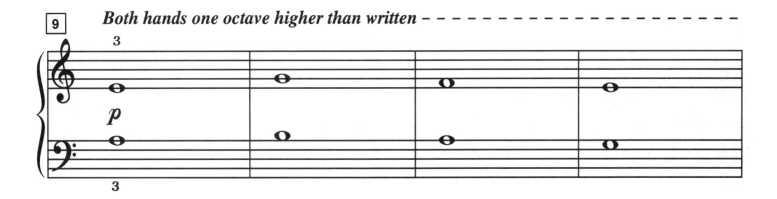

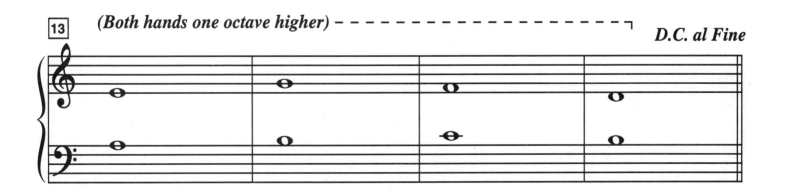

First Waltz

Secondo

Happily

Both hands one octave lower than written

Martha Mier

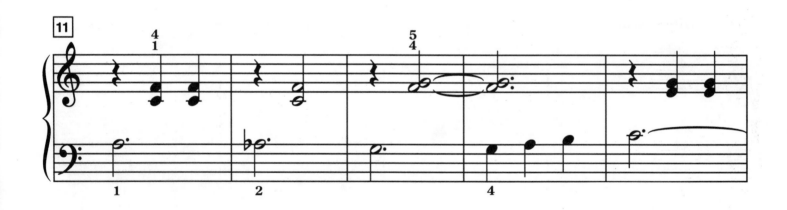

First Waltz

Primo

Happily
Both hands one octave higher than written

Martha Mier

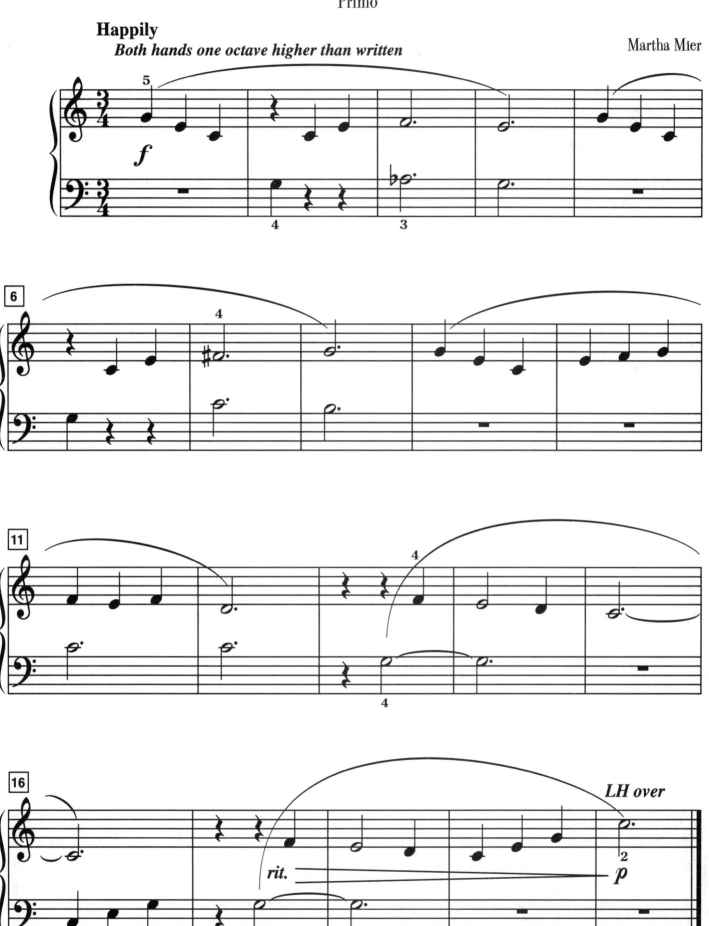

Shoe Shinin' Blues

Secondo

Lazily

Both hands one octave lower than written

Martha Mier

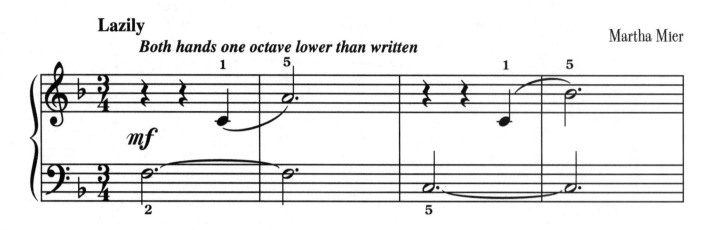

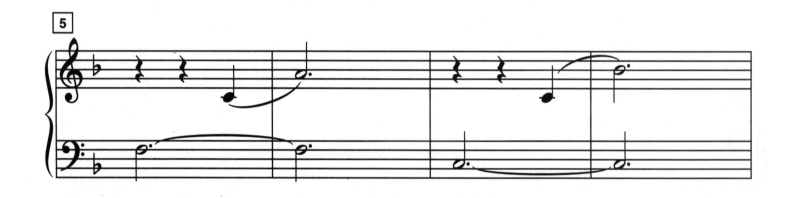

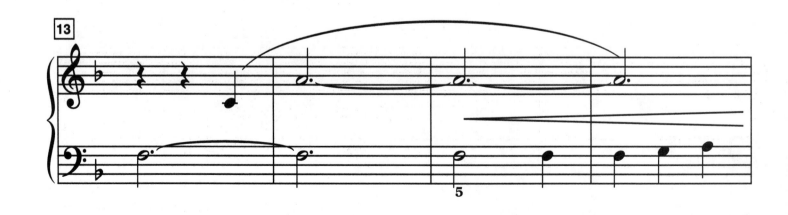

Shoe Shinin' Blues

Primo

Both hands one octave higher than written

Martha Mier

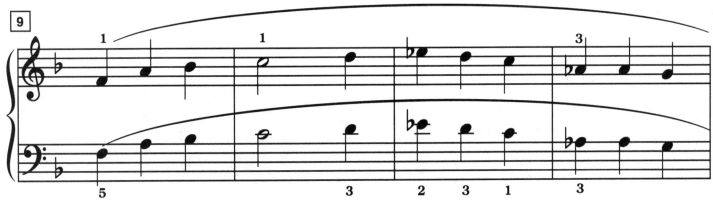

Secondo

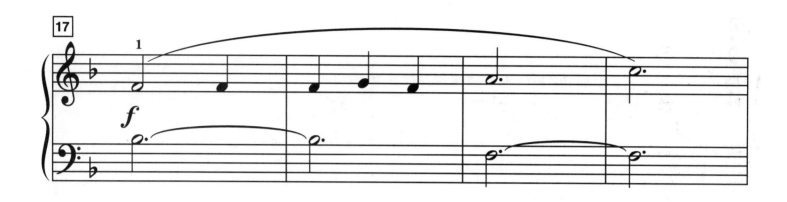

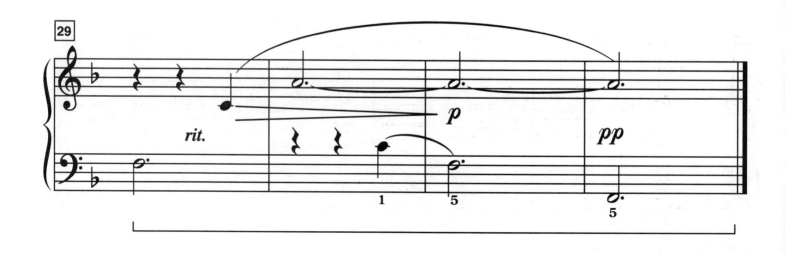

Primo

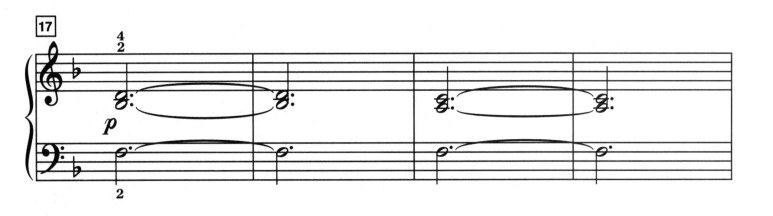

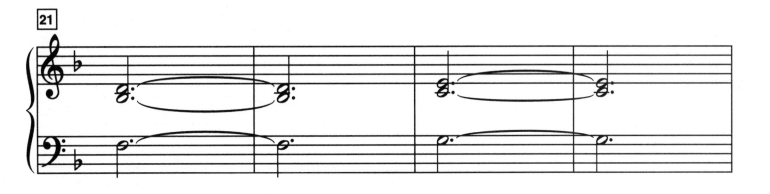

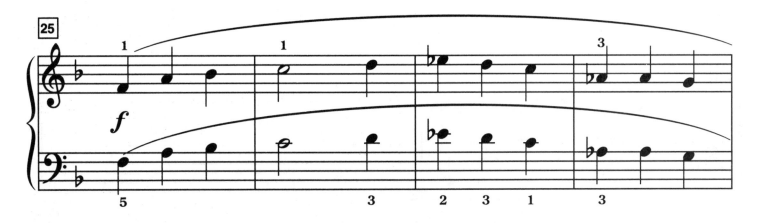

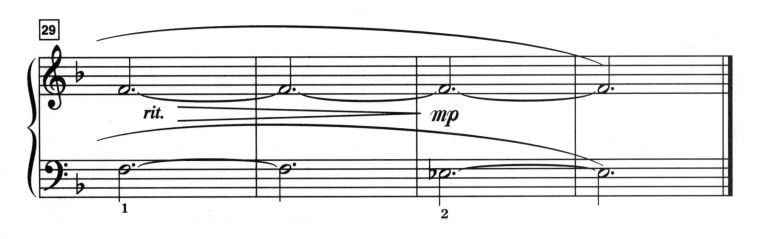

Moonlight Stillness

Secondo

Unhurried

RH one octave lower than written

Martha Mier

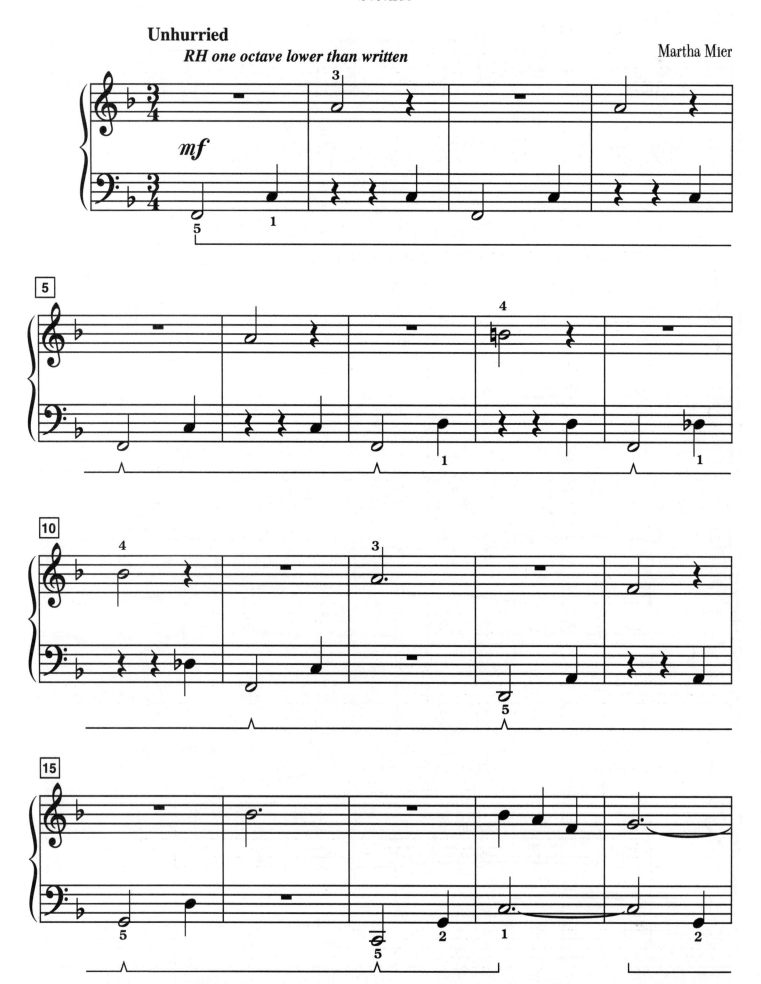

Moonlight Stillness

Primo

Martha Mier

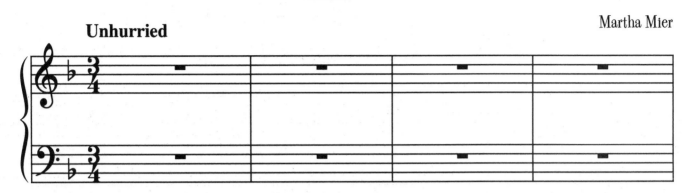

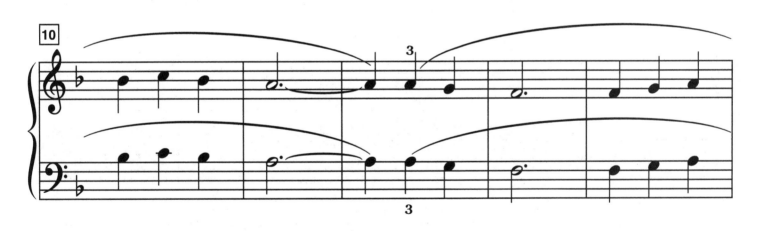

Secondo

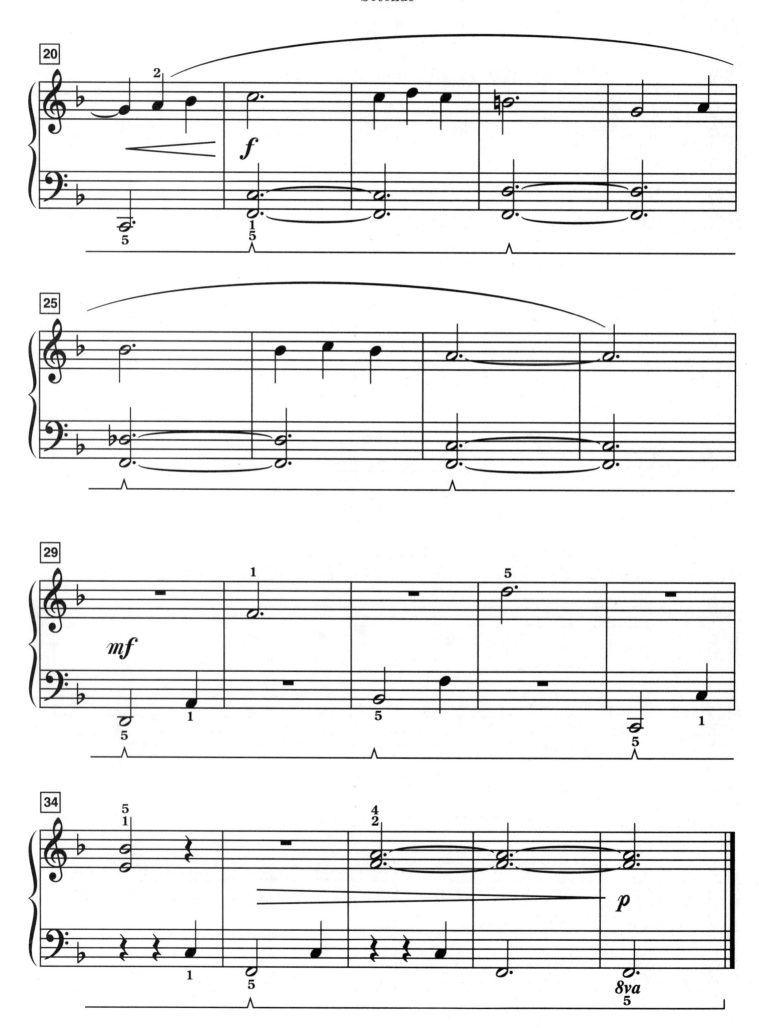

Primo

RH one octave higher than written

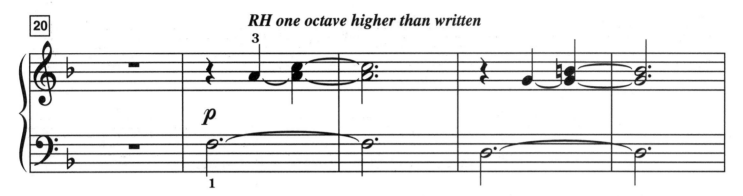

LH two octaves higher than written

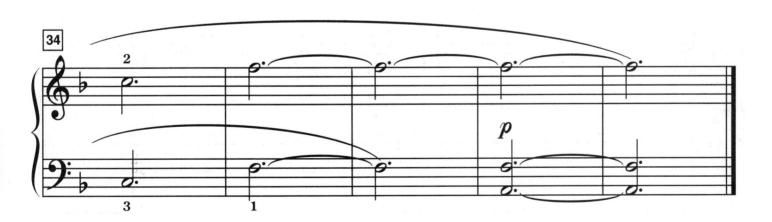

Red Rooster Strut

Secondo

Jauntily

Both hands one octave lower than written

Martha Mier

Red Rooster Strut

Primo

Jauntily

Martha Mier

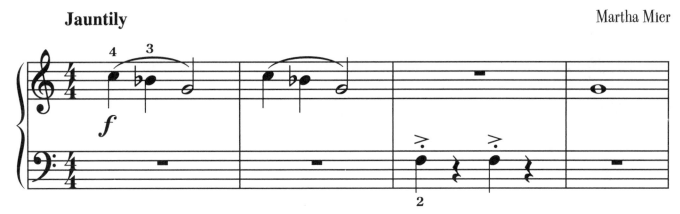

LH one octave higher than written

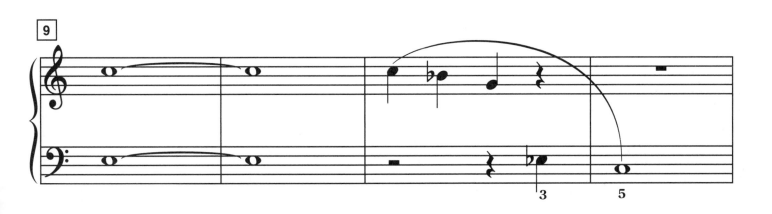

Secondo

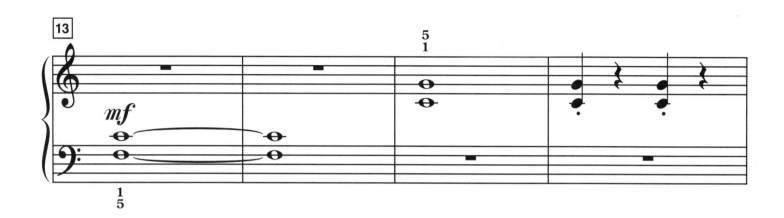

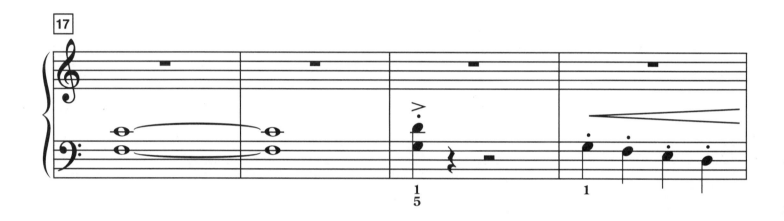

Primo

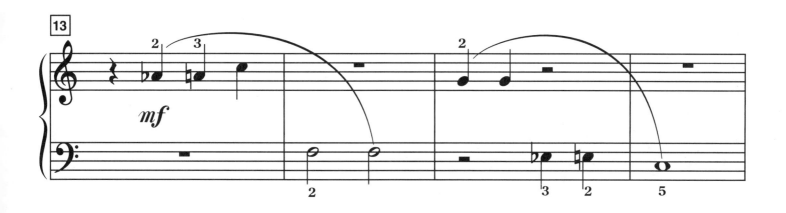

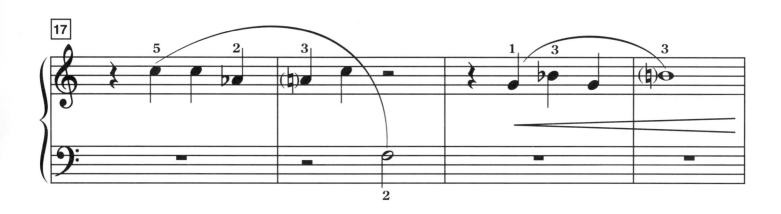

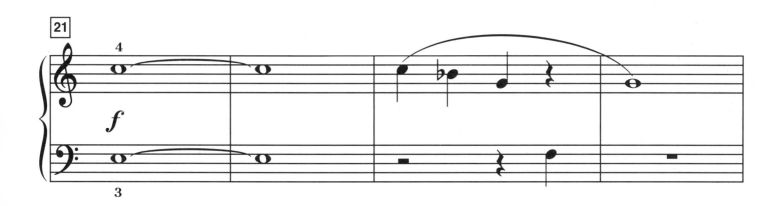

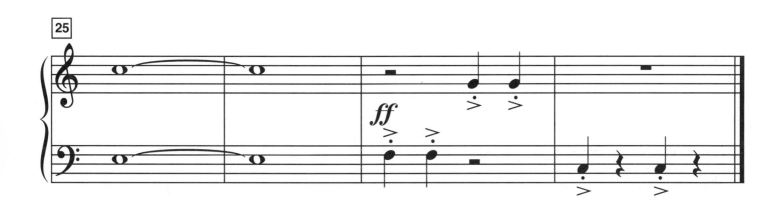